GW01087070

# FRAME IT

**Beverley Behrens**

Series Consultant Editor: Bob Tattersall

## CONTENTS

## COLLINS

# Introduction

Picture framing is often thought of as something to be left to professionals and, in some cases, this is true. However, with patience and a small amount of preparation, you can frame your own pictures at home. This is not only a very satisfying activity, it can make the difference between having the frames you want and having to settle for what you can afford to have done professionally.

There are many framing skills and techniques that the do-it-yourselfer may never learn – indeed, many of the tools of the professional would be too costly for anyone not wishing to make a living from framing. Nevertheless, all the materials used by the professional are available to the beginner and, by using a few simple tools, a high degree of proficiency can be achieved if you are willing to master a few basic techniques.

There are practical (as well as aesthetic) reasons for framing. You cannot hang a picture on a wall unless it has a support, and the picture will soon deteriorate unless it is protected. This obviously applies to valuable paintings, but a photograph, diploma, or some treasured memento may have just as much, if not more, value for you, and you don't want it damaged.

**What else can be framed?** There are so many possibilities: embroidered samplers, posters, the children's drawings, stamps, illustrations from old books, old postcards. Three dimensional subjects such as keys, small shells, butterfly collections and coins can work. No matter what it is, framing will protect it as well as show it off beautifully, so that many old treasures can be pulled out of the attic and take pride of place on your walls.

Above *A mixed selection of prints, drawings and photographs have been arranged together to make an attractive display. Before starting to hang any pictures it's a good idea to arrange them on the floor; you will then be able to experiment.*

Right *This original drawing for a newspaper cartoon has been framed, along with the printed version, in a narrow black frame. Hung with other keepsakes, framed in a similar way, they make an interesting display.*

Below *This lovely old watercolour needed little enhancement. A plain white window mount was used with an old gilt frame.*

3

**Which Frame?**
There are no hard and fast rules about which frame suits which type of subject. A good frame is one that you feel looks compatible with your picture, but the following may be helpful as a rough guide.

*Watercolours* are traditionally framed with narrow, thin mouldings, the size of the mount varying the overall size.

*Oil paintings* on canvas are not usually framed under glass as the reflection will hide the texture and depth of a medium which should be seen in an unmasked state. Either a generous, large moulding or a simple, thin edge are the most suitable.

*Drawings* are treated in much the same way as watercolours. Sometimes it is nice to see the edge of the drawing. In this case, do not frame it with a window mount, but stick or 'tip' onto the mount board. This would give a 'free', unrestricted feeling to the picture.

*Prints, etchings, lithographs and silk-screen prints* are usually framed with a window mount cut just wide enough to show the edge of the print which, if good, should be sharp. Etchings have an indentation running around them made when the damp paper is pressed on the plate. This should also be shown.

*Posters and prints* of the mass-produced type can be treated in any way, but generally, prints look best with a narrow, simple frame.

*Photographs* often look very good with a fabric mount and black and white photographs can take quite a bright, strong coloured mount using a 'no frame' frame or a very modern frame.

*3-D objects* use a 'shadow box' frame.

# Tools & materials

All you need are a few inexpensive hand tools to make basic picture frames, and these will last a lifetime. Here is a list of those that are necessary and the materials you will be using.

The first requirement is a place to work. A good, sturdy table with a flat top (such as the kitchen table) is the best surface to work on. If you are able to walk around it, so much the better.

## Measuring and Cutting

*A mitre box* is the basic tool for cutting the 45 degree mitred corners of a frame. You can buy many different kinds of inexpensive wooden mitre box. However, when picture framing, you cannot start sanding and planing slightly inaccurate mitred corners to make them fit, so, unless you are very practised with a saw, you're unlikely to get the best results with this type of box.

The author recommends a metal mitre box (like the one illustrated) which will cost at least twice the price of the wooden one, but will be worth every penny. It will enable you to cut perfect mitres, and will save many hours of anguish and frustration.

The metal mitre box has two screw holes for fixing it to a work bench but, if you're using the kitchen table, screw the box to a piece of wood and then clamp the whole thing to the table with *G-clamps*. This will be quite firm enough, but don't forget to protect your table with a piece of plywood or chipboard (particle board) first. This type of mitre box comes with complete instructions for cutting the mitres.

You will need a *tenon saw* to use with the mitre box. One with a 300mm blade and fairly fine teeth is best. Try not to skimp on the quality of the saw – some cheap ones can't be sharpened.

Cutting mitres requires the saw to be as sharp as possible. When you feel it's losing its 'bite', you can have it sharpened inexpensively by professionals. Most hardware stores provide this service.

*G-clamps* are useful for holding glued sections together and securing the mitre box to the table.

*A metal tape measure* is more accurate than fabric ones.

## Joining and Nailing

*A tack hammer* is the best weight for pinning the corners of mouldings together.

*A nail set* (or a blunt nail) for recessing the nail heads.

*A small hand drill* is needed to bore holes for the pins holding

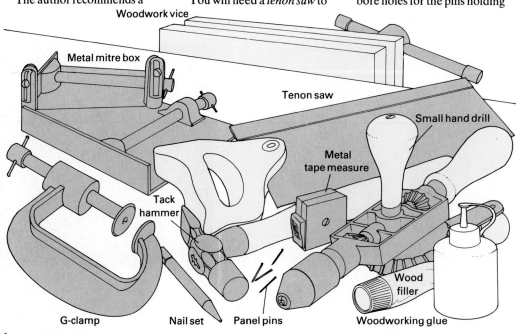

Woodwork vice

Metal mitre box

Tenon saw

Small hand drill

Metal tape measure

Tack hammer

G-clamp

Nail set

Panel pins

Wood filler

Woodworking glue

the frame together when using a very thin moulding. The most useful sizes of drill bit are 1mm and 1.5mm.

*Wood filler* in various colours is used for filling nail holes and scratches in mouldings.

*Woodworking glue* is used on the mitred corners before pinning them together.

*Panel pins* are best for medium and heavy mouldings. Veneer pins are thinner and so help avoid splitting lightweight mouldings. The most useful lengths are 25, 38 and 44mm. A small *woodworking vice* is needed for holding the moulding when joining the corners.

## Finishing

*Fine glass paper and flour paper* are abrasive sheets used to smooth wood mouldings.

*Woodstains* are for changing the colour or darkening wood mouldings. They are widely available and come with full instructions for using and mixing them.

*Sanding sealer* is a quick drying clear primer used to prepare wood for waxing, varnishing or painting. By applying thin coats and lightly rubbing down each one, a smooth surface is built up.

## Mounting

Use a *craft knife* with replaceable blades, which should be kept razor sharp, for cutting mounts and cardboard. If you're serious about framing, you may wish to invest in a mount cutter. These cut perfect bevelled edges and come with full instructions.

*Compasses* are useful for drawing circular mount windows.

*A metal straightedge ruler* is essential for cutting against.

*A set square* is necessary to establish right angles.

*Mountboard* is available in different qualities. For hinged mounts that have a window cut in them, use the best quality. This has a white core that shows when the bevelled edge window is cut. A thinner and less expensive mountboard can be used for backing pictures.

*Double sided tape* is used to attach pictures to the backing mount. As an alternative, you can use stamp hinges.

## Assembly and Hanging

*3mm hardboard* is the best material for the overall backing.

*Brown, gummed tape* is used to seal the back of the picture.

*Picture wire*, fastened across the back of the frame to screw eyes or D rings, gives an adjustable hanging point.

*Turnclips* that hold the backing in the frame are available from art shops.

*Clips* for the no-frame method hold glass and backing together, and are sold at most art shops.

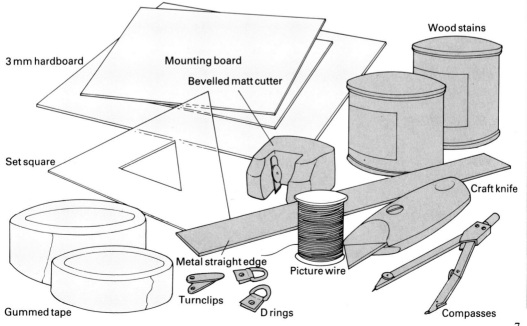

3 mm hardboard  
Mounting board  
Bevelled matt cutter  
Wood stains  
Set square  
Craft knife  
Metal straight edge  
Picture wire  
Turnclips  
D rings  
Compasses  
Gummed tape

# MAKING A BASIC FRAME

Before starting, it will be helpful to become acquainted with the jargon of the framer. The most important part of a picture frame is the moulding. It is on this that your success with framing will metaphorically and literally hang! There are hundreds of different styles of moulding available from picture frame shops or timber merchants. Any wood can be used for the moulding, but some are more popular than others. Basswood is common and an excellent choice for the beginner, as it is light and easy to handle and can be stained or painted. There are also aluminium and plastic mouldings, but these need cutting with a hacksaw (unusable with a mitre box) and can be bought ready cut or in kit form.

all the layers snugly.

You can *make your own mouldings* at home by glueing together strips of architrave (used for edging doors and windows).

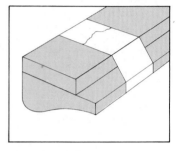

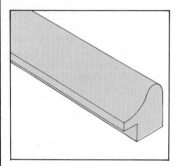

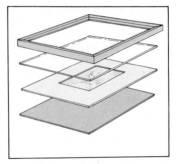

All *ready-made wood mouldings* have a rebate (or rabbet). This is the recess underneath the lip of the moulding that holds everything in place. In the case of oil paintings that need to lie flush with the frame, you won't need a rebate.

Into the assembled frame goes first the glass and then the picture. Finally, the backing board, usually made of hardboard, holds the others in place. When buying your moulding, make sure the rebate is deep enough to accommodate

These won't have a rebate, but you can make your own by glueing a strip of wood to the bottom of the moulding. Hold the strip and moulding together with tape until the glue dries, and then sand the join. This method allows you to make a rebate of any depth. Alternatively, you can ask the timber merchant to cut a rebate into the moulding for you.

## Measuring for the Mitred Joints
When cutting the mitres, work from the external measurements

## How Much Moulding to Buy
Trim the picture you're going to frame, cutting off drawing pin holes and bent over corners. Then attach it to a piece of paper (see Mounting). To work out how much moulding you need, first add the length and width of the mount and multiply by 2. Now, head for the moulding supplier (with the picture) to try out the various shapes, sizes and colours.

When you've selected your moulding, add to your first measurement 8 times the width of the moulding chosen (to allow for the overall dimension of the frame) plus a cutting allowance of 200mm.

You may now have an alarmingly long piece of moulding to carry home. Ask the suppliers to cut it in half – the two lengths will always be sufficient for two sides of the frame.

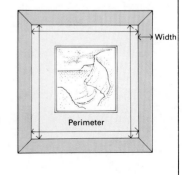

of the frame. To arrive at these, first calculate the rebate size. This is the length and width of the mounted picture plus an allowance of 2mm for clearance. (For instance, the rebate size of a picture measuring 120mm by 100mm would be 122mm by 102mm.)

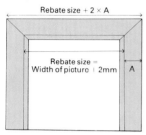

Next, measure the width of the moulding, and from this deduct the width of the rebate. This will give the dimension marked A. The formula for the external measurement of the frame is: Rebate size + 2 × A (the measurement between the edge of the rebate and the outside edge of the frame).

If, for instance, the moulding you've chosen for the picture with rebate size of 122mm × 102mm is 40mm with a rebate width of 10mm, the external frame size would be: 122 + (2 × 30mm) by 102mm + (2 × 30mm).

## Cutting the Mitres

If the moulding you've bought has been cut in half for easy

carrying, cut mitres at each of the four ends. Otherwise, cut two mitres at the middle and one at each end.

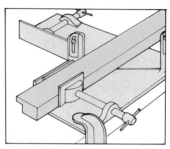

Clamp the mitre box firmly to the table. Clamp the moulding into the mitre box with the rebate side away from you. If you're using a metal mitre box, insert pieces of thin wood or card to prevent the metal from marking the moulding when the clamps are tightened. Also, make sure the moulding is resting absolutely flat on the bottom of the mitre box. If not, the angle of the cut won't be accurate.

Practise cutting mitres with spare pieces of wood and holding them together on a flat surface to be sure you've got the method right before cutting the moulding.

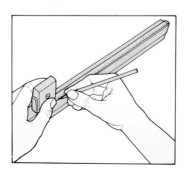

Take one of the lengths of moulding with the mitre at one

end and, using a metal tape measure, mark the external measurement of one of the longer sides on the outside edge of the moulding.

Use a set square to draw a perpendicular line across the edge, making sure the top of the line will be visible when you clamp the moulding in the mitre box. If necessary, continue the line over the edge.

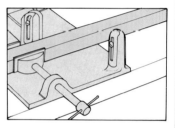

Making sure you will be cutting the mitre in the right direction, clamp the moulding in place and cut the mitre with light, steady pressure.

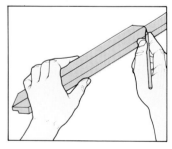

Having cut the first of the longer sides, place it back to back with another piece and mark the length directly. Cut this mitre and check that the two sides are equal length.

Repeat this procedure for the two shorter sides. It's a help to mark the opposite sides of the frame (perhaps one pair as X and one pair Z) so they don't get confused.

## Joining and Nailing

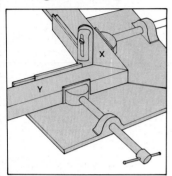

four pieces in the shape of the frame.

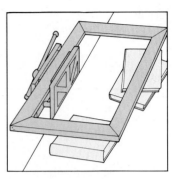

Take one X side and one Y side and position them as if for cutting in the mitre box. Clamp both sides where they form a tight 90 degree corner. Now you will be able to see if they fit well together. At this stage, decide on the position of the pins which, together with the glue, will secure the joints of the frame. For mouldings up to 10mm wide, one pin in each corner will do, but bigger mouldings should have two pins to prevent the joint twisting.

Take one of the longer sides, clamp it into the vice and brush the undrilled end with glue. Butt the end of the adjacent short side (with drilled holes) to the glued end and prop it up so the two sides are level.

When the glue has set enough to be able to handle, place one of the L shapes in the vice and join the other to it, as before. Be sure to support the free ends so the frame is flat while you drive the pins. Clean off the excess glue and leave the frame to dry on a flat surface.

### Making a frame without mitres

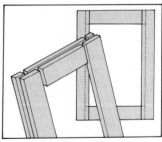

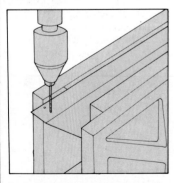

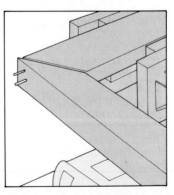

Place the mouldings in the vice and drill holes to prevent the wood splitting – not too near the face or back of the frame, nor too close to the edge of the rebate. Drill the holes in one end of each side only. Lay all

Place the drilled end slightly proud of the other so that the action of hammering in the pins will result in a flush joint. Drive in the pins and sink the pin heads with the nail set or blunted nail. Wipe away any squeezed out glue with a damp cloth and then carefully remove the two joined sides from the vice and place them flat on the table to dry. Repeat with the remaining two sides.

You will need two pieces of rectangular timber moulding, one narrower than the other in order to create a rebate. Glue and pin the two side pieces before cutting them to size. Having then cut them to size, determine the measurement of the top and bottom front pieces. Then measure the narrower back pieces. Glue and pin these together as you did for the sides. You will now have four corners which will butt into each other. These can now be joined in the usual way with glue and pins.

# Finishing

If you have made up your own moulding or bought a ready-made (but unfinished) moulding, you must apply a finish to the frame before inserting the glass, picture and mount.

## Waxing

If you like a natural finish, waxing is ideal. First, sand the moulding very smooth with fine sandpaper or flour paper. A beeswax furniture polish works well. Rub the first coat into the wood with fine wire wool. When the wax is completely dry, buff it with a cloth. Apply a second coat, this time with a cloth, and buff again until you have a smooth sheen. On carved or beaded mouldings, you can get the wax into the crevices with an old, soft toothbrush and buff with either a soft shoe brush or clothes brush.

## Staining

Wood dyes and stains are available in a large range of colours as well as the traditional wood tones, such as walnut, oak, mahogany etc. The colours can be mixed to give in-between shades as well, so a whole artist's palette is available. However, you must stick to one type of stain when you mix them. There are three types: *water based, oil based and spirit based* and they aren't compatible with each other.

Be sure to test the stain on a scrap piece of the same wood before starting on the frame.

After sanding the frame smooth, build the colour slowly, using several coats of diluted stain. This helps avoid more absorbent parts of the wood becoming darker than the rest.

After staining, follow the manufacturer's instructions about finishing with wax, varnish or shellac polish.

## Painting

Mouldings that are to be painted should be sanded really smooth. A couple of coats of sanding sealer, rubbed down with flour paper in between, will take up any imperfections in the grain or minute gaps in the mitres. When the wood feels silky to the touch, it's time to apply the first coat of paint. Most types of paint can be used, but make sure it is compatible with the sealer (if in doubt, test on a scrap piece of moulding).

Aerosol cans of paint are very handy for frames as they avoid brush marks in the corners. Follow the instructions on the can and apply several thin coats rather than risking drips and runs.

It isn't always necessary to feel you have to cover the whole frame with paint. A line of paint along a beading or a recess edge picked out in a colour can be just as effective.

When doing this, it's a good idea to mask one or both edges of the line to ensure a good, clean edge. It's sometimes

easier to do this before joining the frame together. Silver and gold paint used this way can make an ordinary frame look very expensive.

*Spattering* is a traditional finish used by framers. This is adding speckles of a darker colour to the final painted or varnished surface.

Dip a toothbrush into the oil paint that is diluted with white spirit (mineral spirits).

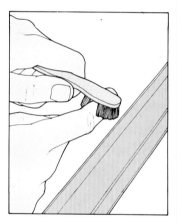

Shake off any excess and then run your fingers across the bristles so flecks of colour are flicked onto the frame. Test the effect on a newspaper first.

There are other special effects which can be achieved with paint, such as rag rolling, sponge stippling, graining etc. These are described in the companion book PAINT IT.

Whether staining or painting, keep your tones compatible. The frame should not be competing for attention with the subject it is surrounding.

Having made the frame and mounted the picture, all that remains is to assemble them with the glass and the backing.

Glass makes an amazing difference to the finished frame. Besides being necessary for protection, it intensifies the colours of the picture. *Non-reflective glass*, which eliminates all reflection, has a flattening effect; sometimes more obvious than the reflections it is trying to prevent. It is considerably more expensive, so unless you have a problem with reflection where you intend hanging the picture, ordinary *picture glass* is best. This is of a standard thickness and is much thinner than window glass.

For beginners, the simplest way is to go to your local glazier, framing shop or hardware store and let them cut a piece of glass to your exact measurements. This will be the rebate size less 1mm each side for clearance. Although it is not difficult to cut glass, the amateur will probably not have the space to store large amounts of thin glass safely, if there are small children around, the last thing you want is for them to be playing in the glass chippings. Also, there are no large savings from buying large sheets of glass and cutting off what you need.

However, if you have a piece of glass from an old frame and want to cut it smaller, you can buy a glass cutter at any DIY shop. This should be dipped in white spirit before each cut as it helps to keep the wheel running smoothly and the cutter sharp. Smooth the edges of the cut glass with wet emery cloth.

Lay a piece of felt or towel on the table and place the glass on top. Use the set square and straight edge to score a line all the way across the piece. Be sure the scored line goes right to the edges.

Slide a thin strip of wood beneath the glass with one edge along the line and press down on either side, snapping it in two. It's difficult to cut off edges of less than about 25mm, so if your glass is only slightly too large, it's easier to buy a new piece the right size.

## Tips

The cut edges of glass are razor sharp! If you're framing with the no-frame method, ask the glazier to grind and polish the edges.

Having bought the glass, you can now cut a piece of hardboard to the rebate size and you are ready to assemble.

## Backing
The backing is easier to buy cut to size by your supplier, as you probably don't want to store a large sheet of hardboard. Most DIY stores will cut neatly and square to your measurements, but offcuts are cheaper, so if you have a piece you want to cut smaller lay it on the table with the smooth side up.

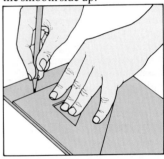

Measure and use the set square to draw the lines to be cut. If necessary, use a longer straightedge with the square.

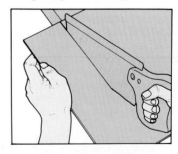

Keep the edge of the table as near to the cutting line as possible, and support the overhanging part with one hand. You can use the tenon saw with quick strokes, being careful not to let the part you're holding sag, or the last part of the cut may tear.

If you find that you can't keep from tearing the bottom surface of the hardboard, don't worry as this edge will be covered by the tape when the frame is assembled.

If the tearing out at the edges is too serious, place a waste piece of hardboard or thin plywood underneath and cut through both pieces. Also, if you're cutting off a large piece, put a piece of wood under the sheet after you've started the cut to help support the work.

## Assembly

Clean both sides of the glass thoroughly, using warm, soapy water. Then, rinse off and dry with a clean, lint free cloth.

Clean the mount face and remove all specks. Any pencil marks can be gently rubbed off with a soft eraser.

Place the frame face down on the table, insert the glass into the rebate, followed by the picture and the hardboard. Check to see it's absolutely clean; you may have to repeat the cleaning process to be rid of all the specks.

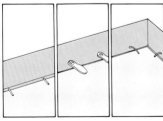

If the rebate is deeper than the sandwich, you can tap veneer pins into the back of the rebate every 75mm to hold everything together.

If the backing is flush with the

frame, use turnclips.

Alternatively, drive pins into the back of the frame and bend them over the backing.

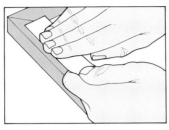

Finally, to prevent dust getting inside, seal the back edges with gummed paper or masking tape.

## Hanging

Attach screw eyes or D rings each side, about one third of the way down from the top of the frame. Make sure the screws are long enough to hold, but not so long that they come through the front of the moulding.

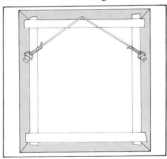

Thread picture wire through the rings twice and twist back up. The wire should come just below the top of the picture when fully stretched.

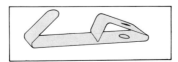

The usual method of hanging is to use picture hooks. These have

hardened pins to be able to penetrate masonry or wood and will support most pictures on most walls. For heavy pictures or mirrors, use mirror plates.

However, if the wall is too hard for the pins, or if it's hollow and the picture is too heavy, there are picture hooks that use screws.

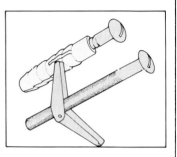

In solid walls, a hole is bored to take a plastic plug, into which the screw is driven; and, for hollow walls, there are fittings that expand behind the wall and grip when the screw is tightened.

To measure where the hook should be, get a helper to hold the picture in the right position and then make a small mark on the wall at the middle of the top of the frame.

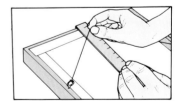

Then place the picture face down and measure the distance from the top of the frame to the wire, when fully stretched. Place the hook on the wall the same distance below the mark and either drive in the pins or mark the hole for the screw.

# FRAMING WITH A MOUNT

A mount increases the overall size of picture and also, by giving space between the picture and frame, lets the picture 'breathe'. There are basically two types of mount.

The simplest is a plain piece of card or *mountboard* onto which the picture is mounted (or 'tipped'). This serves as a backing for the picture, as well as leaving an area around the outside.

The other type is a *hinged mount,* in which the picture is seen through a window cut through a second card on the front. Hinged mounts should be used for pastels, drawings and watercolours as they would be damaged if they were in direct contact with the glass.

Mounts are made of special card called mountboard. This is stiff and thick and yet cuts easily. Mountboard is available in a wide range of colours and shades and, when a window with a bevelled edge is cut in it, the white inside of the card creates a miniature frame that gives depth to the picture. There is also a thinner, less expensive mountboard available for the simple mounts that won't have windows cut in them.

Not all small art shops will stock a large range, but a little searching around will usually provide the right colour for your picture.

But, how do you decide which is the right colour? The subject to be mounted must be considered quite carefully. Take the picture with you when buying the mountcard. The colour should tone with one of the colours in the picture itself, or at least be complementary to the overall tone. Avoid a very strong colour that would compete with the picture, the mount should only highlight and enhance it.

Mounts can be decorative in themselves. You can cover them with fabric, paint designs on them or draw simple lines around the windows. Two or three mounts of different colours and with different window sizes can be placed on top of each other to give an even greater feeling of depth to the picture. Also, a single mount card can have several windows cut in it, enabling a number of pictures to be arranged in one frame.

Once you've mastered the basic technique of making a mount, try experimenting with your own ideas.

Left *Limited edition etchings 'tipped' onto dark brown mounting card.*

Above *The blue of the embroidery has been echoed in the mount, on which a fine line has been drawn for further emphasis. The wooden frame has been hand-painted with various shades of blue matt paint.*

Above left *This window mount is covered with self-adhesive shelf paper. White lines have been drawn round both edges of the mount and serve to accentuate the dried ferns, which have been allowed to tumble over the edge of the mount.*

Above right *An attractive and unusual way to display a lovely old lace tablemat and a pretty lace handkerchief. In one case a fabric-covered mount has been used with a simple wooden frame; in the other a simple coloured mount has been framed with a hand-decorated frame.*

Right *A junk shop find. Old watercolours sympathetically treated with oval mounts and dark stained wooden frames. The choice of a dark colour accentuates the delicate painting.*

# Making a hinged mount

If you decide to use a hinged mount, then the mount should be your first concern. Choose a colour that is right for the picture and determine the overall size of the mount before buying the moulding.

To give the right effect and show the picture to its best advantage, keep the mount as large as possible, but always remember that about 6-9mm will be lost in the rebate of the frame. Dimensions are, to some extent, a question of personal preference but, as a general rule, narrow margins tend to give a pinched-in, tight look, and very small pictures can benefit from extra wide margins. Usually, the smaller the art, the wider the mount and vice versa. Also, it is best to avoid a repetition of widths, such as the same width moulding as width of mount.

Mark the cutting lines for the window very lightly in pencil on the front of the mount board.

You are now ready to cut the bevelled edge. Don't attempt to do this until you've practised cutting on a spare piece of mount board!

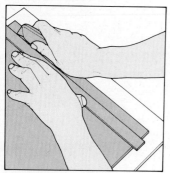

Two L shaped pieces of card are useful for deciding how much of the picture is to show. Make the size of the window slightly smaller than the picture itself, for a neater finish.

Using an old piece of card underneath so as not to blunt your knife, take your straightedge and cut the mountboard to the area decided on. Use the set square to make perfect, right angled corners. To ensure the board is truly square, measure the diagonals to see they are the same.

Next, cut a mount back of thinner, cheaper card, exactly the same size.

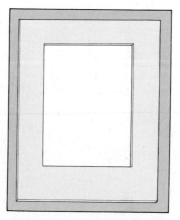

When measuring for the window size, make the bottom margin slightly more than the top and sides. This will make the picture appear central in the frame when it's hung on the wall.

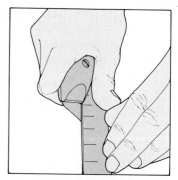

Using the metal straightedge to guide your knife (or mount cutter), score lightly but firmly along the line, holding the knife at an angle of 50 or 60 degrees and pulling it towards you. Then, score again with the knife at the same angle, until you've cut right through. It may be necessary to ease the tip of the knife into the corners to free the cut out part completely. If there is any fuzziness on the bevelled edge, a gentle rub with flour paper will eliminate it.

To complete the mount, hinge the back and front together with sticky tape. Position your picture so that the desired area shows through the window. When you're completely satisfied with its position, attach the picture permanently to the back with double sided tape or stamp hinges. These should be stuck as close as possible to the top edge of the picture.

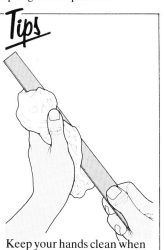

Keep your hands clean when touching the mountboard. Wipe the straightedge before cutting. Pencil marks are easily removed with an eraser or bread, but greasy finger prints are hard to remove.

## Fabric Covered Mounts

There are times when the texture of a fabric can greatly enhance a painting or drawing. You should always use a hinged mount because of the problems of attaching paper to fabric. Any fairly thin fabric, such as *linen, lawn, moire, gingham, muslin, satin* etc. can be considered.

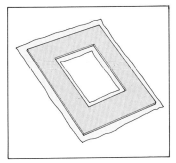

After cutting the window in the mount in the usual way, cut a piece of the fabric a little larger all round. Make sure the grain of the fabric is running straight and glue it to the mount front. You can use ordinary fabric adhesive, but the aerosol mounting adhesive from art shops is best. Spray it over the whole surface of the card.

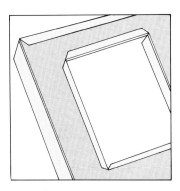

Make diagonal cuts to the corners of the window, and then turn the mount over and glue the edges to the back of it. You can trim off the pointed ends to leave enough fabric to keep the edge stuck down.

Attach the mount back, position the picture and finish in the usual way.

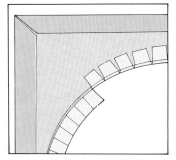

Oval and circular mounts can be covered by making cuts towards (but not quite reaching) the edge of the mount. Then, fold and glue the flaps one at a time, pulling each one to keep the fabric tight and to prevent the ends of the cuts from showing on the edge of the window.

## Special Mount Finishes

There are many ways you can decorate a mount. If you intend to do this, it is a good rule to use the 'no-frame' principle (discussed later on) and to use the decorated mount with a simple subject, such as a portrait or a simple drawing.

*Painting* a mount with a simple pattern can be very effective. Coloured inks are suitable for this. An easy decorative touch is to draw lines around the mount windows with a ruling pen. These are inexpensive and well worth having as some of the thicker inks, such as white, black or gold flow much more easily through this sort of pen. Ordinary fountain pens tend to get clogged. With a ruling pen you can also draw lines of different widths, but this takes practice.

*Stencils* can be bought ready made or you can make your own. Designs are best kept simple to avoid distracting attention from the subject.

There are shops that sell beautiful *decorative papers – marbled, coarse textured, Japanese rice paper –* any of these, even *wallpaper,* can be stuck to the mount and carefully cut out with the craft knife. If you do plan to cover the mount, you can use the cheaper type of mountboard.

Experiment also with *pressed flowers, sequins, cutouts* from old scrapbooks and *lace.* Whatever decoration for the mount you choose, make sure it is firmly stuck on with the appropriate adhesive.

## Circular and Oval Mounts

These are much easier to cut out of paper or thin card than out of mountboard. If you want the bevelled edge that you only get from mountboard, you could ask a picture framer to do the mount cutting for you. Some art shops sell ready-cut oval and circular mounts. The type of mount cutter used by professional framers is not worth investing in unless you intend taking up framing for a living!

To cut mount from paper or thin card, you can use templates supplied from art shops, or look around for anything you might have at home first. The kitchen is a good place to start, a plate or bowl will serve the purpose just as well.

With your craft knife you can cut directly against a template

but if you are using a plate or bowl it is probably simpler to mark the circle in pencil first and then very carefully cut along the line with the craft knife. If you plan on making several circular mounts, you can buy a compass cutter from art shops.

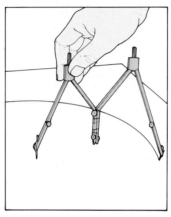

A compass will make a perfect circle, and two compasses, the pointed end of one where the pencil would be in the other, will give a greater span.

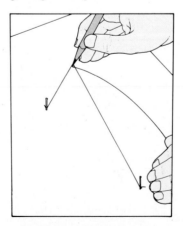

For the oval, two drawing pins and a loop of string will enable you to draw ovals of various proportions.

## Mounts with More than One Window

If you have several small drawings, postcards, stamps or photographs, the answer may be to cut a mount with several windows. Any number can be happily incorporated into the frame, but the planning and laying out needs to be done carefully. First, find the best arrangement on a sheet of paper, grouping the subjects for the best effect. Cut the paper to the overall size.

When you've made your final decision, mark the position of the corners of the windows or cut them out of the paper. Then lay the plan on top of the mountboard and keep it in place with clips or small pieces of tape taken around the back. When you're absolutely sure the paper can't slip, prick through the corners of the windows into the mountboard. Then remove the paper and lightly pencil the lines to connect the corners. Cut the bevels as before.'

# FRAME KITS

There are several different types of frame kits on the market. The most common are made of aluminium and sold as pairs of sides, so that you buy two packs of two for each frame. They start quite small and go up in size by about 50mm at a time, so you should always be able to find two pairs of sides to suit your picture. Many variations in size are possible, and this could be helpful if you were planning to clad a whole wall and wanted a feeling of unity.

When using these, you will still have to fit your picture to the frame, make a mount and backing and have the glass cut. However, you will have the mitres already cut for you and also the necessary angle plates and screws for joining the corners together. They come with full instructions, are very simple to assemble and very strong at the corner joints.

Various frames for canvasses are also available in kit form. There are other kits that come complete with glass and backing. These can be made of aluminium or some are unfinished wood to be finished any way you choose.

**No frame frames**
Some pictures look better when there is no frame to close them in. A frame isn't always essential, indeed, why not use the wall on which the picture will hang as the frame! A picture sandwiched between a backing board and glass and held together with clips is particularly suited to today's style of simplicity and high tech. Kits are readily available and can be assembled in minutes. However, they are also easy to make yourself from many varieties of clips and brackets available from art shops, hardware stores and framers. Often this is less expensive than buying in kit form.

Above *A simple aluminium frame which was easily assembled from four pieces and a few clips. The mount was available at the same supplier.*

Above *No-frame frames used in a kitchen to protect simple prints and drawings.*

Above *Perspex box type frames are available in many sizes. Here they have been used to display family photographs. By arranging on a simple grid more boxes can be added as and when they are wanted.*

# Other frames

**Passe partout** and other similar tapes are a quick, inexpensive and easy way of framing small pictures or snapshots. Children's paintings or drawings also are ideal subjects for this method. There is no actual frame, but the tape used to bind the edges provides the illusion of one. A 'no-frame' kit is the simplest way to use this method, or you can buy the glass (be sure to ask for the edges to be polished). Cut the hardboard backing piece to the same size, or have it cut by the supplier.

The glass, backing and mount (optional) are held together by the passe partout tape.

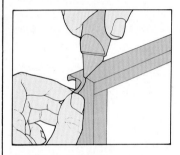

Carefully trim the ends of the tape flush with the corner, making sure the glass and backing won't show.

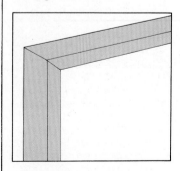

Then, either leave the front edges overlapping, or use a straightedge and knife to cut

through both layers of tape. Remove the off-cuts and you have a mitred corner.

## Strut Back Frames

Strut back frames are most commonly seen on mantelpieces or dressing tables. Any ordinary frame can be made into a strut back by cutting a tie shaped piece of hardboard about two thirds the length of the frame.

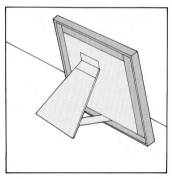

This is attached to the backing board by either a light cabinet hinge or fabric tape. A piece of cord or ribbon is then glued on to the strut and the back of the frame top prevents the strut from opening too far. If the frame is metal, small pads of felt can be stuck to the bottom to prevent it scratching the furniture.

## Fabric Frames

If you're good with a needle, you probably have scraps of dressmaking material or furnishing fabric left over. These can be used to make fabric frames, perhaps to fit in with your decor. The method of doing this is basically the same as for covering a mount with fabric.

First, cut out the shape of the frame in thick card. Lay the fabric on the card and position the mount over it, and draw

around the window, leaving a good margin to fold around the edges. Cut out the window in the fabric.

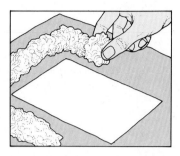

At this stage, you could pad the fabric with a layer of cotton wadding to give the frame a bit more thickness.

Make the diagonal cuts almost to the corners of the window, fold the edges around and glue them to the back of the mount.

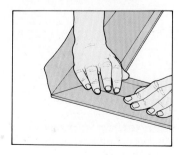

Now, make diagonal cuts to the outside corners and fold the

edges around, glueing them to the back. Try to keep equal tension on the fabric to avoid creases on the front.

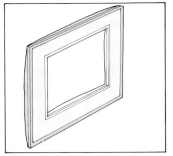

To finish the back, cut another piece of fabric a little smaller than the mount and cut the window large enough that the edge of the fabric won't be seen from the front. This backing can be sewn around the edges, but it's easier to glue it over the whole surface.

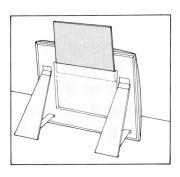

Finally, cut a piece of felt slightly larger than the picture and glue just the sides and bottom edges to the back of the mount. Now you have a sleeve into which you can slide the picture.

To turn this type of frame into a strut back, you could make two struts, and fix them either side of the window.

Another method of making a frame is to make a basic wooden frame from the plainest moulding, such as clamshell or half round. Using the same method as for covering a mount, glue fabric directly onto the frame using spray adhesive.

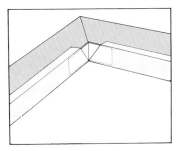

If the frame is deep and you have trouble getting the fabric to cover the inside corners, glue small strips of the same fabric along the edge at the corners before folding the main edge around.

## Other Finishes

If you have a frame with a very simple, plain moulding, you can attach a variety of things. *Shells, strips of bamboo*, almost anything goes. It's not unheard of to bake frame-shaped pieces of bread dough in the oven!

## Making a Shadow Box Frame

Shadow boxes are used to display three dimensional objects, such as a collection of *butterflies, shells, coins, and old fans, tapestry work, textiles* – in fact anything than won't lie completely flat.

The box is created by using a moulding with a very deep rebate, so that there is a large space between the glass and the back of the frame. Decide the required depth of the rebate as

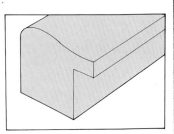

follows: if the object is 12mm thick, add the thickness of the glass (3mm), the thickness of the mount (2mm), and at least 5 mm for the clearance between the object and the glass = 22mm. Add another 6mm for safety.

Measure and cut a piece of mountboard and cover with fabric such as felt or velvet.

Then, measure for the moulding, cut the mitres and make the frame in the usual way. Measure for the glass and insert this into the frame.

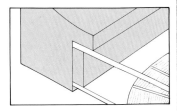

Now, you need four strips or 'fillets' of wood to hold the glass in place and create a second rebate for the mount. Cover the fillets with the same fabric as the backing board, as they will show once the frame is assembled. Glue the fillets to the side of the rebate in the moulding, making sure they touch the glass.

The object can be attached to the mount with pins, glue, small strips of velcro or it can be sewn.

When the glue has set, insert the mounted object, followed by a backing board, and finish in the usual way.

# Old frames

There are many ways you may come across old frames – junk shops, auctions, jumble sales – perhaps there are a few dusty ones lurking in the attic. When you're looking at one, don't be put off by the subject in the frame, try to imagine the frame around a picture of your choice. By now you should be armed with enough confidence and know how to set about making a new mount to fit an old frame or re-cutting its mitres.

A word of caution, if you find one that you think may be valuable, take it to an antique shop, a good picture framer or a valuer for his opinion before you start to chop it up. This could well apply to gilded or carved frames.

Right *A large collection of old frames of various types and sizes look very attractive hung together in a rather random fashion. To achieve something along these lines you must be willing to spend a lot of time planning how the pictures best relate to each other and the whole – there are no hard and fast rules, you must simply experiment.*

Above right *A marvellous way to display school pictures, holiday snapshots, wedding photographs and other personal momentoes. By hanging the pictures very close one gains an overall effect which is immediately interesting, but which also allows any old frames (regardless of style or condition) to hang alongside more modern ones.*

Above *This beautifully renovated collection of old frames are all slightly different; however, hung together they complement each other and are further linked by the flower prints they hold.*

## Metal Leaf Gilded Frames

Assuming the frame is in reasonable condition, i.e. with no large chunks missing, a clean up with some acetone or white spirit may be all that's needed. Work on small sections at a time, dabbing the area dry with an absorbent rag to see how things are going. Use white spirit (mineral spirits) if you suspect the frame is painted and you just want to clean it. Use acetone if it is gilded (or you want to find out) as paint will come off, but gold will be unharmed. If you remove a layer of gold paint, you can simply apply another coat. With a gilded frame, a light coat of lacquer will protect and seal its surface, after cleaning. Aerosols of clear lacquer are sold for this purpose.

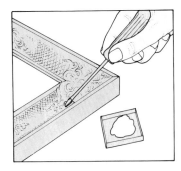

If there are only small bits of moulding missing here and there, these can be filled in with car body filler, which can be shaped and sanded when set.

## Wooden Frames

If the frame has been *painted* first clean with white spirit (mineral spirits) and, if it's not too chipped, sand and re-paint. Use a suitable undercoat.

If the frame is *polished* and simply dull and grimy with age,

clean it up with methylated spirit gently rubbed on with fine wire wool. It can then be waxed. If you want to darken the colour, there are tinted waxes you can use.

Remove any old brown paper by sponging with water, but take care not to soak the wood.

It may well be that an old wooden frame has wobbly mitres. Here you may decide to take the frame apart and re-join or even re-cut it. Try to ease the corners apart by hand.

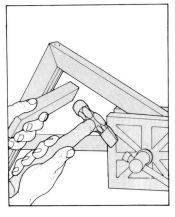

If that doesn't work, clamp one side of the frame in the vice and gently knock it apart with a hammer. Use a block of wood to protect the frame. Try to take it apart in the direction of the old pins, as it is then less likely to split. Unfortunately, it's not always possible to see from which side of the joint they were put in. Have a good look at all four joints; maybe you'll see how one was joined and you can assume the other three were done in a similar way.

Once apart, the nails can be pulled out with pliers, and the holes filled with a mixture of fine sawdust and wood glue.

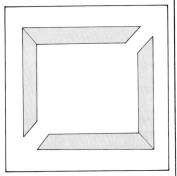

If the mitres are sound, but you want to make the frame smaller, then you need only to cut through two corners diagonally opposite each other. Don't use your tenon saw to cut through the nails at the corners, use a hacksaw instead.

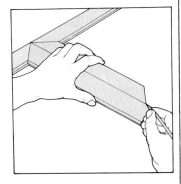

Measure the length of one side as if you were making a new frame, and having cut one mitre, use it to mark the opposite side in the usual way.

**Tips**

If you are stuck for ideas with an old frame try turning it into a mirror. The size would be no problem as mirror glass can be cut to fit any frame.

# Mirrors

Mirrors are possibly the easiest of subjects to frame; they require no mount and can be framed in an endless variety of styles – from heavy ornate gilt to the simplest pine. By their very nature one's eye is drawn to them and this is an occasion where you could safely let your imagination run wild on the kind of frame used. Highly decorated frames, made of fabric or shells, for example, can all be equally stunning. The prettiest mirrors by far are those with a bevelled edge, but unfortunately they are much more expensive.

On a practical note, remember that mirror glass is at least twice as heavy as picture glass and, therefore, a frame for this purpose must be sturdy enough to support the extra weight. It may even be necessary, in the case of a large mirror, to reinforce the mitre joints with metal corner plates attached to the back of the frame.

Above *This simple mirror was made from a square of hardboard, with a circle cut out of the centre, covered with a remnant of printed velvet. A small mirror was then stuck onto the back.*

Right *A simple white painted wooden frame has been made for a mirror and then thin strips of white painted wood have been stuck on top of the mirror, so making it resemble a window. A useful idea for cheering up a dark corner or a small room.*

Left *Tiny shells of different colours have been stuck onto the mirror to make an attractive design and different shells have been used to make the flowers. Any mirror could be embellished in this way – either a modern plain one or perhaps an old one which has begun to lose the silver around the edges.*

Below *The frame of this old oval mirror was too damaged to repair, so velvet was stretched over it and stuck down firmly at the back. A ribbon was stuck to cover the join and add further interest.*

# DISPLAY

Sometimes it's hard to place your pictures where they will have the maximum effect. Over the mantelpiece or over the bed are two places where anyone can hang a picture without difficulty but, all too often, they're put up on any bare expanse of wall without much thought as to their size, colour or effectiveness. The result is that they are often 'lost'. A common mistake is that pictures are hung too high – you should be able to look into a picture without cricking your neck. Also, pictures are not for looking at only when you're standing – take care that they're not out of sight when people are seated.

If you have more than one small picture, consider grouping them close together on one wall. They will have much more impact then if they're just dotted around randomly. You can either frame them in a similar style and colour, or let them contrast with one another, some quiet, some vibrant, some narrow, some wide etc. The secret of successful grouping is to form a type of grid into which your pictures will sit.

Taking four or five pictures, for instance, plan an imaginary cross through the centre of your group. The width of the cross should ideally be about the same size as your mounts, and the bottom of the highest pictures will be level with the tops of the lowest. To this system, more and more pictures can be added, keeping the spaces between them the same. Try out your arrangements on the floor first, otherwise someone in the family will end up with aching arms!

Right *These prints have been hung very close together as they complement each other and are more effective hung as a pair. For this reason they were not put in heavy frames, which would have had the effect of separating the subjects.*

26

Left *A series of modern flower paintings have been simply put behind glass to maintain the uncluttered look and so allow them to be hung close together.*

Bottom *Simple no-frame frames have been used for these colourful graphics, which look good just leaning against the wall.*

Consider hanging pictures in places other than the sitting room. A kitchen or bathroom shouldn't be ruled out because of steam and moisture. Posters, prints or magazine pages (i.e. anything not too precious) can liven up these rooms. Children love pictures in their rooms, but remember to hang them low enough for the children to enjoy them.

Try to balance pictures with objects near them. You may have a piece of wall space that calls for a particular shape of picture, such as a long narrow one in the space between two doors or two horizontal ones along the side of a bath. A small print will be lost on a large expanse of wall, but may be just right in an alcove or between two pieces of furniture. Similarly, a big picture will look dramatic on a large expanse of wall that is uncluttered by other pictures or ornaments.

Stairs offer a picture-hanging challenge. Here they're seen either going up or coming down – a dramatic one at the end of the climb could be stunning; or place a group of quiet ones at the beginning of the stairs to be contemplated while standing still.

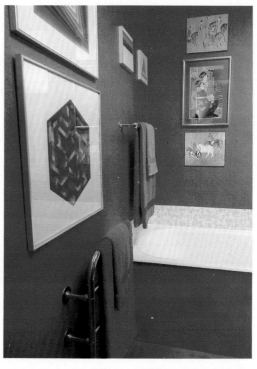

Above right *The pictures in this bathroom have been hung in groups of two or three for maximum effect. Don't put anything valuable in your bathroom or kitchen in case the steam damages it.*

Right *A group of pictures hung on a simple grid. The three on the left set the grid and the others, all slightly different, follow it as closely as possible. A nice way to display this type of work.*

Far right *The pictures here have been hung to follow the line of the stairs. This is much easier when they are all the same size, but when they vary considerably do give yourself plenty of time to experiment.*

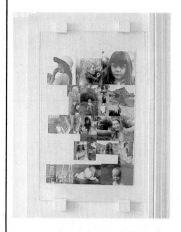

Top left *Blocks of wood fixed to the wall support a back sheet, mount and glass and allow them to slide out so that the photographs can be changed.*

Centre left *A simple wooden frame with wooden backing makes a perfect display for a collection of metal numbers and signs.*

Bottom left *This simple appliqué has been mounted on a size of board that allows for a small border of the backing fabric to show around the edge.*

Above *The four sides of this wooden frame were covered with satin before the frame was assembled. This makes the frame part of the appliqued satin picture it surrounds.*

# TOP TEN TIPS

**1.** When cutting the moulding, always cut the longest side of the frame first. This way, if you make a mistake, you will still have enough to make the shorter sides.

**2.** Use short, quick movements of the saw when coming to the end of cutting the mitre. This helps avoid splitting the wood as the saw breaks through the bottom of the moulding.

**3.** When masking off an area for painting, don't forget to remove the tape before the paint dries.

**4.** When glueing the mitres, always make sure all traces of excess glue are wiped away with a damp cloth before it dries.

**5.** Don't use your tenon saw to cut aluminium mouldings or nails in old frames. Use a hacksaw.

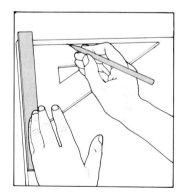

**6.** Never assume anything is square – even sheets of mountboard. To establish a true square, place your straightedge along the side and lay the set square against it to draw a right angle. You will then have one true right angle from which you can obtain the other three.

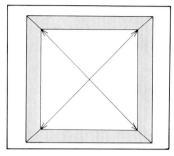

**7.** To check a frame or mount is square, measure the distance between diagonal corners. They should be the same.

**8.** Don't hang unglazed pictures over a radiator. The rising dust and dirt will soon affect them.

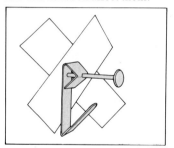

**9.** When hanging a picture, tape on the wall will help avoid damaging the plaster.

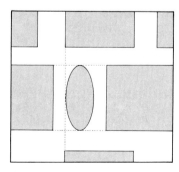

**10.** If you are grouping pictures and want to add an oval, treat the oval one as a rectangle lining up the widest part.

## Safety Tips

**1.** When using sharp edged tools, always keep all parts of your body behind the cutting edge.

**2.** Don't leave tools where children could play with them. That goes for nails and pins, too.

**3.** Always wear heavy gloves when handling glass with rough edges.

**4.** To minimise fire risk, finishing materials should be stored in clearly marked containers with tight fitting lids, and out of reach of children.

**5.** Never underestimate the weight of a picture or mirror.

**6.** Always ensure there is good ventilation when using paints and solvents.

**7.** If you are using the kitchen as your workroom be extra thorough when sweeping up splinters of glass etc.

**8.** Don't leave pieces of moulding with protruding nails lying around. Either tap nails out with a hammer or remove with pliers.

**9.** Never leave glass lying around. Find a safe place to store odd pieces you may wish to use at a later date.

*Author*
Beverley Behrens
*Series Consultant Editor*
Bob Tattersall
*Editors*
Dek Messecar and Alexa Stace
*Design*
Mike Rose and Bob Lamb
*Picture Research*
Liz Whiting
*Illustrations*
Rob Shone

*Beverley Behrens* trained as a designer and has been involved in many aspects of art and interior design & decoration.

*Bob Tattersall* has been a DIY journalist for over 25 years and was editor of *Homemaker* for 16 years. He now works as a freelance journalist and broadcaster. Regular contact with the main DIY manufacturers keep him up-to-date on all new products and developments. He has written many books on various aspects of DIY and, while he is considered 'an expert', he prefers to think of himself as a do-it-yourselfer who happens to be a journalist.

*Picture Credits*
*Pictures from Elizabeth Whiting Photo Library*
Photographed by Steve Colby, Clive Helm, Graham Henderson, Neil Lorimer, Michael Nicholson, Spike Powell, Tim Street-Porter, Jerry Tubby
Cover Photography Clive Helm

*The Do It! Series* was conceived, edited and designed by Elizabeth Whiting & Associates and Rose & Lamb Design Partnership for William Collins Sons & Co Ltd
© 1984 Elizabeth Whiting & Associates and Rose & Lamb Design Partnership

First published 1984
Reprinted 1986, 1987
9 8 7 6 5 4 3 2 1

Published by William Collins Sons & Co Ltd
London · Glasgow · Sydney · Auckland
Toronto · Johannesburg

ISBN 0 00 411919 3

Printed in Spain